echoes of the heart:

passionate declarations

barry siegel

Dedication

I am grateful to all my friends and family and many strangers along the way who have encouraged me to share my words with others.

I am especially thankful to my dear friend Brian for his loyal support and assistance in putting this book of poems together.

Finally to Sheila, my best friend, lover, and wife, for her devotion, time, energy, inspiration and care she has given me for the past nine years. I am truly a fortunate man.

barry

A Note About Dates
Beneath each poem, at the right, is the date each poem was written.

A Note About Organization
Living most of my life in the Midwest, I've had the opportunity to observe, feel, and then reflect on the four distinct times of the year, physically, certainly, but more importantly emotionally. Thus… the table of contents format.

Table of Contents

Table of Contents - 2

Table of Contents - 3

For Me... an introduction

I sometimes wish I could write with a flare,
with words I don't know and words I can't spell.
I sometimes wish I could write fifty poems of laughter and joy,
instead of the hundreds I write about hell.
I sometimes wish I could stretch my imagination
and write about the future as well.
I sometimes wish I could write some poems of purpose and trust and
reason.
I sometimes wish I could write each day in a particular season.
Could I write of mayhem and treason?

Instead,
I write mostly of heartaches and heartbreaks and sad times that each
of us feels.
I write mostly of relations and troubles and injustice and how each of
us heals.
I write mostly of promises broken and prejudice and dishonest,
disloyal deals.

But,
I do write about courage and I do write about hope,
and I do write about love and its might.
I do write about splendid places I've been to
and describe each interesting sight.
I do write about people who fight through the darkness
and finally end up in the light.

And,
I write about fears and tears and mirrors and wild uncontrollable
cheers.
I write about time and space,
and how we journey from the days through the years.
I write about parents and siblings and peers.

I write about now, I write about inside, I write about you and me.
I write about nature, I write about passion, I write about what is free.
I write about life and death, about good and bad, about what I hear and see.

I write to create, I write to stay sane, I write and explore with my heart.
I write when I fall apart.
I write when I'm wrong, I write when I'm mad,
I even write when I don't know where to start.
I write about beauty and brains and kindness all wrapped into one.
I write about us and all that we have, I write about how we have fun.
I write about you, "My rock and roll angel," about you my warm, shining sun.

I write honestly and simply with words a youngster would know.
Perhaps they will make you understand, perhaps they will make you grow.
Maybe they'll make you stop hurting, maybe they'll force you to get up and go.

I sometimes wish, I sometimes dream.
I sometimes cry, catch my breath, then I scream.
I sometimes run, I sometimes take a chance, I even sometimes sleep.
I sometimes take it easy, I sometimes take it deep.
I sometimes crawl, I sometimes turn, I sometimes take a leap.

Sometimes the words come easy, sometimes they're hard to find.
Sometimes they need to be pulled through, sometimes they just unwind.
Sometimes a process flows, sometimes it's such a grind.

But. . .always JUST ME. . .THROUGH ME. . .FOR ME.

61801

2

Fall

Change/Contemplation

The Shepherd's Flock

Tracing the lines of your life,
coloring red white and black, the stops along the way...
> What is it we're after?
> What is it we need?
> Where do we go from here?

A small decision turns into an acute change of direction,
this is right, this feels good, this is my year, my time has come.
And you hope.
> And you try.
> And you pray.
> And you do.
Wouldn't most do it differently if they could?

Tracing the lines of your life,
coloring red white and black, the stops along the way...
Take out the horror, the loss, the regrets and leave what's left.
> If only we could.
> If possible, we would.
> If tomorrow, we should.

Time soars at the late autumn of our lives,
no more days, only months and years.
Sweet, precious time... do now what you once would do later.
Take a stand where you once would turn slightly away.
Love freely where you once would keep one foot on the ground.

Footprints that wash away with the slightest rain,
or shadows that follow us from here to there.
> First... a friend like a brother,
> then... a father like a friend, passes.
The line remains strong, though less.

With each loss comes an increase in awareness.
> Of time.
> Of frailties.
> Of fears.
> Of love.
> Of self.

Tracing the lines of your life;
coloring red white and black, the stops along the way…
The harshness of winter,
>with a sleigh ride
>under the clear night's moon
>on a desolate country road
>tucked away in a small corner
of the ice cold and gray December days.

The awakening of spring,
>with its reborn sounds
>and sights
>and thoughts
>that stir all the emotions,
none more than passion.
Yet, tucked away in a corner of the spring flowers
and sweet whispers of nature that abound, lies a realization,
>that all is not the same
>and some things will never be.

The youth of summer,
>with its laughter
>and splashing
>and kissing
>and experimenting
>and first loves
>and forever sunsets.

Yet, in a corner of the heat lies a spot,
where the tan turns to disease
>the heart cannot bear to break one more time
>and where the intense fever turns
into jealousy, revenge and rage.

Finally, the appreciation of fall,
>with its cool wonderful wind
>and its glorious array of yellows and browns
>and reds and greens
>and its resolve with feelings
of more understanding and accepting.

Yet, in a small corner of the forests' full and hearty wonders
lies the knowledge,
        that soon this will become the bitterness of winter
        and that the future is not now as long as the past.

Tracing the lines of your life,
coloring red white and black, the stops along the way...
        dismissing the unimportant
        holding on to the love
        dreaming of the possible
        discussing tomorrow
        living today.

My future line is painted in pink...
        pretty and warm
        sometimes spicy
        sometimes hot.
        Pink.

One long, always beginning,
        (one hopes) never ending line....
        this line of life.

One line, millions and millions of paths....
        the Shepherd's flock.

22397

5

Walk around and observe the peoples' state of mind,
even if you look real hard and you look real close...
        you still may never find.
The smiles are gone. The pain is in the eyes, not quite as kind.
The rules are twisted inward and the pages are unlined.
The world and all its forces are suddenly entwined.

Real heroes, but a few...
icy veins now running blue.
Politicians politicking, speaking right on cue,
if you think it, the same old thing can turn out to be something new.
Look into the sky at night and sense what's really true.

Oh, speck of lights!
Oh, fear of nights!
Oh, time of plights!
Oh, tear of fights!
Oh, wind of kites!

Yesterday, today and tomorrow no different,
but the (places, the faces)
(the crimes, the times)
(the seasons, the reasons)
(the names, the shames)
(the ages, the pages)

Oh, God of pay!
Oh, glimpses of day!
Oh, memories of May!
Oh, spectrum of gray!
Oh, density of clay!

Walk around and observe the people's state of heart,
fear, violence and confusion… fuel the new art.
Good and bad push further apart
The blood always warm on the devil's chart
You better plan to show your love…
and right now is the time to start

5…4…3…2…1

101802

A Viewpoint

You know you can lose your vision, but you still can see.
You can be locked in chains, but you still feel free.

You look around and through to find out who you are.
You stay within yourself, but you wander far.

Time isn't holding us, in fact, it's opening some doors.
Between the lines, you'll find some secret drawers.

Some have this feeling they've been here before.
The mind is our passage, while the heart is our core.

As we age, we discover what was already there.
We water the garden. We walk hand in hand.
We watch the leaves fall in the cool autumn air.

Down the road through the darkest alley,
through the thickest forest,
through the tallest mountains,
through the overcrowded highway,
through the deepest ocean,
through the tiniest grain of sand...
you'll find reason and kindness, truth and fairness, love and faith.

You'll find all that was missing and find all that there is...
for once, and for all, you'll find yourself.

8300

Ask Yourself

If you were at your own funeral, what would you see,
four hundred pairs of sad eyes or about twenty-three?
How about all the things that you've acquired so far,
you know; the house, the leather, the diamonds, the car?
When the service is over and the days become years,
do your friends and family still think of you with sweet tears?

If you went to your own funeral, what would you say,
"Here was a man who lived a full life each and every day?"
If you went to your own funeral, what would you feel,
is this a dream, or could this be real?

If you went to your own funeral, what whispers would circulate?
"With kindness and compassion, he lived not long enough."
Or, "The way he treated others, he deserved his ultimate fate."

If you went to your own funeral, what would you do?
Would you open your heart to each one there
and let them look straight through?
If you went to your own funeral, what would you hear,
a poem of friendship and hope, or a dark tale of selfishness and fear?

If you went to your own funeral, what would you see,
four hundred pairs of sad eyes or about twenty three?
You've been released from your body, you've been finally set free.
If you went to your own funeral, would you see me?

9900

Mind Into Matter

Inadvertently, his mind switched gears,
he thought about the minutes, he thought about the years.
He thought about the thousand smiles that journeyed into tears.

He took a ride and came upon a pond amongst the trees.
He thought about the dollar bill and how it never frees.
He thought about his throbbing heart and how it always sees.

He left his car and took a walk and wandered far away.
He thought about tomorrow as though it were today.
He thought about the bitter cold and wished that it were May.

He started heading back as the darkness settled in.
He thought about her morning smile and how that made him grin.
He thought about his treasured art, a number made of tin.

Finally back at home again, he welcomed in the light.
He thought about the sky above and humanity's miraculous plight.
He thought about love and hate and death and joy and fright.

Inadvertently, his mind switched gears,
He thought about sweet romance and all the truth in mirrors.
He thought about his comfort zone and how he'd face his fears.
He closed his eyes just long enough to hear his father's loving cheers.

123001

Gather Around

Mothers and fathers, gather around.
Listen very carefully, and don't make a sound.

Here are the gifts you can give to your children.
Here are the gifts, and they are free.
Show them a rainbow they can make by themselves,
and show them the strength and the bend of a tree.

Show them an ant, and a hawk and a mare.
Show them what's wrong and what's right and what's fair.
Show them the dawn and the sun at high noon.
Show them the stars and autumn's harvest moon.

Give them discipline and freedom.
Give them hope, give them space.
Give them knowledge and choices and provide a safe place.
Give them forgiveness and give them time.
Give them oceans to swim in and mountains to climb.
Give them hugs, give them kisses,
Give them encouragement and wings.
Give them parades and charades and playgrounds with swings.

Mothers and fathers, these and many more,
Won't cost you any hardships, won't cost you a dime.
You won't have to worry, nor commit any crime.

Money's of no concern,
don't you get it, don't you see?
Love is the answer, love is the key.

LOVE IS THE BLESSING THAT CAN ONLY BE FREE.

61601

12

Sheep

Welcome to my world in the middle of the night. . .
        quiet runs its course,
the lake is still,
the moon aware,
the body still at rest.
Think, write, read, watch . . . move about the room,
a pattern designed to exhaust.

Now close your eyes and count out loud, the millions keeping pace...
        and the millions still who chase,
        and the millions unable to finish the race,
        and the millions all with one face,
        and the millions of daydreams entangled in lace,
        and the millions of species in our endless space,
        and the millions quietly sharing their grace,
        and the millions uninvolved . . .
            their existence without a trace!

101802

Undercurrent

Behind the whispers.
Beyond the limits.
Beneath the humor.
Before the consequences.
Between the fears.
Beside the symptoms.

Mumbles, murmurs. . . simmering, flickering.
Seconds ticking away. . .change reinventing itself.

Imagination of the mind.
Emancipation of the body.
Fascination of the spirit.
Infatuation of the heart.
Transformation of the energy.

Undulated.
            Unparalleled.
                        …Undercurrent.

102202

Facts

Try again.
Give, will receive.
Only right now.

This trilogy bought to you...
by reactions and tears,
        by risks and fears,
        by setbacks and cheers,
        by moments and years.

102402

Questions

Can you stop the rain?
Can you catch the wind?
Can you leave all of your troubles behind?
Can you bring out the sun?
Can you paint the sky blue?
Can you find the time to unwind?

Will you crawl, walk, then run?
Will you jump through a hoop?
Will you kiss your sweetheart hello?
Will you show that you're sorry?
Will you take a stand for what's right?
Will you find the strength to tell temptation no?

Have you dreamed about Heaven?
Have you visited Hell?
Have you strolled amongst the trees hand in hand?
Have you looked deep inside?
Have you helped out a friend?
Have you ever made love in the sand?

Do you do as you say?
Do you hide all of your pain?
Do you think enough before you act?
Do you believe in a god?
Do you follow your heart?
Do you live your life matter-of-fact?

Are you true to yourself?
Are you still having fun?
Are you kind, respectful, and fair?
Are you reaching for that star?
Are you knee-deep in mud?
Are you likely to take on a dare?

Should you council the young?
Should you provide for the old?
Should you shelter the ones who are lost?
Would you trust a stranger?
Would you hide the truth?
Would you help protect freedom at any cost?

Now for your answers, but first one more question...
Is today your very last day?
Since you don't know that answer, since you can't buy another...
Try to live it a much better way!

102402

The Distance

Who do you want to be...
Some Hollywood star doing anything for fame?
Or, some bigwig politician disgracing his name?
How about that sports hero not trying her best?
Or, that pinstriped C.E.O. who failed each lie detector test?

Who else do you want to be?
The clergyman hiding abuse behind his collared shirt?
Or the rock and roll idol forever covered in dirt?
Perhaps that noted writer of novels, once again quite depressed?
Or, that portrait of wealth, lonely and stressed?

Instead of another, how about being just a better you?
You can change some things you used to do.
You can still be better even if you are good.
You can do what you want, not just what you should.

How about more smiles, more hugs, more sweet romance?
How about more walks, more talks, more song and dance?
The past is past, tomorrow way ahead,
But exactly right now, your blood deep red.

Time soars by silently, destinations turn into new starts.
Love of self.
Love of life.
Love of others.
Love's universal in-between...
THE DISTANCE OF OUR HEARTS

11702

Childhood Straight on Through

Expectations rarely met...
you give, but do you get?
The whole world is one big mess...
Power and money, the causes I guess.
Just look around at all the faces
and at all the unimportant chases.
Live with enough, love as much,
the silent voices we seem to touch.

"Kill the children, kill them all..."
even one peaceful day on this earth, I just cannot recall.
A handshake, now some legal prose. . .
open arms that now close.
Slow the brain, pump the heart,
pull together what was once apart.
Tiny ant, great big tree. . .
you are both a part of me.

Listen closely, if you will.
Listen closely, just until.
Listen closely, life's no thrill.
Listen closely, Jack and Jill.

112102

Invisible

The minds behind the faces in front of the camera on the
photograph.
The thoughts behind the actions in front of each house on the
photograph.
The blood beneath the skin in all of us, lying next to us, across the
oceans on the photograph.
The dots connecting us, reinventing us, coming after us...
all colors sizes and shapes...
on the photograph.

The tears behind the smiles, the fears inside of us,
the storms surrounding us, those around before us
on the photograph.
The sky above us, the earth beneath us,
the life besides us, the structures made by us
on the photograph.
A thousand stories, a thousand choices, a thousand hellos and good
byes.
Thrilling moments, grand celebrations, unforgettable horrors on the
photograph.

Expose the images, impose your beliefs... all eyes see differently.
Intentions masked, realities captured, glimpses of innocence caught
by surprise.
Rumors now confirmed
on the photograph.
Daydreaming... imagining... conceiving... forgetting... believing.
In focus... blurred... indistinguishable.
The minds behind the faces, in front of the camera on the
photograph.

Ready or not, smile and say cheese.
Here we go... 1 2 3.
Memories crystallized... mysteries remain... truths confessed...
inside the border... along the edge... within the frame.
All that's INVISIBLE on the photograph.

112402

About Today

I read about the couple's daughter,
disfigured and disabled in just about every way.
But through the miracle of love,
she somehow managed to face each day.
I heard about two guys I knew,
their bodies couldn't fight anymore.
Strong and well some time ago,
they said good bye and locked the door.
I looked about and saw the faces of loneliness, stress and grief,
only a very few kind souls would offer any relief.
I thought about all the world,
and how sad its state of mind.
The search for peace journeys through our hearts,
and truth is what we'll find.

I closed my eyes and thought of you,
then finally started to unwind.

112602

She, Me, We

She need not wait for what she wants,
she need not wait at all.
She need not wait for the sun to rise,
she need not wait for the stars to fall.

She need not wait for her heart to burst,
she need not wait to forgive.
She need not wait for a dream come true,
she need not wait for death to live.

She need not look down at the road too far,
she need not look at the past.
She need not look at the local news,
she need not look at love as though it won't last.

She need not look at what others have,
she need not look away nor judge.
She need not look down on those without,
nor hold an unnecessary grudge.

She need not give away all of her secrets,
she need not give away all her worth.
She need not give into abuse nor injustice,
she need not give away her rights from birth.

She need not give ignorance another excuse,
she need not give her dignity any compromise.
She need not give and expect,
she need not give into money's tempting lies.

She need not be anyone but herself,
she need not pray for riches, but for health.

She need not fall victim to fame,
she need not love another with shame.
She need not hide her joy nor her pain,
she need not live her life in vain.

12502

22

Sideshow

What goes on offstage?
Time's on whose side, and at what age?
Inside, outside, it's all the same cage,
Sometimes a smile can hide the rage,
Experience colors the words on a page... Sideshow.

The whispers behind the masks,
the preliminaries, the crew, the after-hours tasks.
Beneath the surface, between the clicks, karaoke, candlewicks.
Around the world magic tricks,
consolation games vampire ticks... Sideshow.

The regular grind,
something easy to find,
almost exactly the same kind.
Finish up, then unwind.
No spotlight here, the simple mind.

History's ghosts.
A rhythmic flow.
Just passing through... Sideshow.

1503

Present Tense

A brief encounter,
a lapse of memory,
a curiosity, of sorts.

A cloudy blur of white and gray.
Fact or fiction?
How long ago?
An involvement, of sorts.

Looking for clues,
listening for reminders,
vocalizing for affirmation.
A dream,
a wish,
a nightmare.
Perhaps a reckoning, of sorts.

A pleasure, a discovery.
An admission, a fear.
A notion, a secret.
A joke, a prayer.
Grace or Hell,
crystal or rock.
A passage, of sorts.

Long forgotten,
once again,
over and over.
A sanctuary, of sorts.

1503

What Is

The tone of his words. . . the aftermath.
The silence after the bullet. . .the tragedy.
The color of her skin. . . the prejudice.
The apple of his eye. . . the pedestal.
The phone, the car, the crash. . .the senselessness.
The first cry. . .the innocence.
The first try. . . the courage.
The first goodbye. . .the sadness.
The trust in his eyes. . .the temptations.
The world now and then. . .the bloodshed.
The money, the greed, the power. . .the entitlement.
The sky, the earth, the waters. . .the wonderment.
She volunteered to lend a hand. . . the priorities.
The lifetime gift of discovery. . .the passion.
The body aches the mind untangles. . .the aging.
The intimate search for peace. . .the truth.
The heart flutters and sparkles, reaches and accepts. . .
        the love.

1603

Blood

And the world spins around
and the people cannot be found
and the world spins ahead without any sound.
The people killed all other forms
then the people killed themselves.
Nothing left now
but machines, sky, earth and water.
Nothing left now
but the smell of greed, deception, hate and war.

And the world spins
empty with sadness and fear.
And the world spins
Uncertain, uncaring... a collision is near.
No trees, no mountains, no flowers in May.
No feathers, no seashells, only dreams made of clay.

No second chance, no moonlit dance.
No cosmic trance, not one harmonious circumstance.
And the world spins
into a new dimension, a new path, a new mode.
And the world spins
out of control... swirling into history
into the vastness of what was once.

And the world spins
flagrantly discordant, discontent, diminished...
and forever defunct.

1803

The Blending

A moment in time,
no reason no rhyme.
A moment in tune,
another none too soon.

A moment of truth,
a moment of prayer,
A moment to find,
a moment to dare.

A moment to bend,
a moment to ascend.
A moment to reveal,
a moment to heal.
A moment of acceptance,
a moment of repentance.

A moment in love,
a moment to know.
A moment of wonder,
a moment to glow.

A moment to unwind,
a moment in November.
A moment in nature,
a moment to remember.

A moment of you.

32303

Winter

Struggle/Connection

Actual

Some folks doing business,
some folks playing games.
Some folks barely eating,
some folks naming names.

Others take advantage,
some others lie in pain.
Others flash their hollow gold,
some others die in vain.

Some folks dancing wild,
some folks at the grocery store.
Some folks caged inside,
some folks engaged in deadly war.

Others creating their own art form,
some others down on their knees.
Others inhaling the early spring,
some others upside down in trees.

Some folks teaching youth to wonder,
some folks growing old too fast.
Some folks forgiving an unhealed scar,
some folks dreaming peace at last.

Others following the mandates of hate,
others paint their hearts deep red.
Others smile hello,
others missing are likely dead.

All others close their eyes. All others do not feel.
All others turn their backs. All others are not real.

    No one is left.

33003

Guide

When it's all said and done, when push comes to shove.
When the meek inherit, when the hawk learns from the dove.
When the shit hits the fan, when the pigs take flight.
When the eyes tell a lie, when you climb from the brink to the light.

When the effort is made, when the rules are broken.
When the dam cannot hold, when the words of love are unspoken.
When the circus comes to town, when life is no more.
When the itsy-bitsy spider, when trouble knocks on your door.

When the land cannot grow, when the heroes fall apart.
When the wind fiercely blows, when the end is a start.
When forgiveness is asked, when a smile cannot hide.
When the games are for money, when the damage is inside.

When the dawn turns to dusk, when rust turns to gold.
When your spirits fade away, when you have someone to hold.
When innocence is lost, when crime doesn't pay.
When seldom is heard, when you've just lost your way.

When it's not a matter of time,
when death do us part.
When you tell the truth,
when your guide is your heart…   then you'll know.

4503

Splattered Blood

The approach is distinctive, the connection on fragile ground.
The wind close ahead, language conveyed without any sound.
A struggle, a compromise, an emotional choice,
screams, horrors... but not your voice.

Time three-dimensional, your heart jumps in vain.
The image is merely a shadow, each tear drops in pain.
Crowded streets capture the pulse, the finish is just another start.
The rope wraps around you, you're still intact but you are coming
apart.

The smiles are hard to come by, the gold all melts to rust.
Your music needs no audience, innocence to exclamation. . .
coronation to dust.
Close your eyes, turn around, or just look the other way.
Neon lights welcome you inside, history and the future are mirrors of
today.

The Queen of Spades is the devil's bride.
Secrets are many, answers but a few. Way too many die.
The last laugh is hollow, the next promise a lie.
Knock-knock... who cares? Hello... good-bye.

Growing pains, growing old... growing up way too fast.
One day you're first... someday you're last.

NOAH'S FLOOD, VIRGIN MUD, SPLATTERED BLOOD

41403

31

Interpret This

Someone else's imaginations may be, to you, very real.
The nightmare next door, reaches down then out, for only you to feel.
You scream, but no one hears.
You cry, but shed no tears.
After some time you lose control,
you know you've dropped into some very deep hole.

The space is divided by color alone;
first amber, then violet, then silver, then bone.
Silent and tempting, you move then you wait,
you wonder if this place is your eternal fate.
Candles and cobwebs, seaweed and sand,
under me the sky, over me the land.
Somewhere in between, I pass through then return,
about how I got here, there is no concern.

My neighbor's horror in the middle of the night,
involved her eyes that could not see the light.
A witness to violence she could not leave behind,
a moment's peace, an hour's sleep. . . neither could she find.
I floated inside each pattern, each hue,
finally, at last, I have a clear view.
I was inside her body, numb and in pain,
I needed to know if I was insane.
Was her mind playing games or was her heart facing fear?
Could she find the courage to look in the mirror?

I woke up and stumbled to the window across the room.
There was no house, just a plot… and an unmarked tomb.
An angel appears and whispers my name.
Some sad things have happened, but you're not to blame.

91800

32

We = Far Too Many

We read the headlines with a tear in our eye.
We push down on the pedal with a heavy foot.
We grab the dollar for more than it's worth.
We beg forgiveness with razor blade thoughts.
We tend to our pleasures with endless detail.
We seek approval from a dissident audience.
We race the clock, but to no avail.

We jump into a screen and lose ourselves.
We barricade our senses with bricks of steel.
We puncture our promises with deceit and excuse.
We determine our fate by luck and deed.
We love best by extension and reception.
We choose our heroes by their fame and fortune, not their spirit or intent.
We pray with our fingers crossed and our hands tied.

We turn our eyes elsewhere, as if wrong were right.
We treat our elders as if we will not become one ourselves.
We are wind, sun and storm.
We are dots connecting sky, land and water.
We walk on eggshells, as our self-respect wanes.
We wait for contact, as if it were only a one-way path.
We magnify our differences, while we ignore our similarities.

We hide faintly behind our smiles, though naked with a single tear.
We blink, and twenty years have passed.
We look at life inside out... we look at death outside in.
We close the door, but we rarely nail it shut.
We aren't... we are... we are not.
We are but one of all kinds.
We are just a particle of it all.

We are but a mountain of heart, within a speck of dust.

112005

33

Journey

Starting over… what's the matter?
Just some longer steps up the ladder.
Trouble is, the time is shorter,
one foot already outside the border.
Sixty years and I'm still here,
the easy pace is never near.

Business as usual… money, money, more.
Masked in diamonds, but still a whore,
paying homage at the devil's door.

Changing me to make a buck.
Never again, I don't give a fuck.
Struggling hard to keep some hope,
test my will, then try to cope.
Three A.M and still awake,
eerie rumblings in the lake.

Where to go… what to do?
Outside grey… inside blue.
Holding on with dried-up glue.

Push through the darkness, pull down a star.
Now secure your heart so you can't fall far.
It's not what you have, it's who you are…
A back seat driver in a rental car.

72705

Jugglers, Clowns, and Thieves, Oh My!

Most are so busy they've forgotten how to slow down.
"Not enough hours in the day," they say.
"Where have the years gone?" they ask.
"Why can't we get ahead," they lament.
Isn't it strange? Isn't it true?
All this behavior hasn't made a happier you!

Turn on the TV, ninety channels or more.
Every other corner, another video store.
Kids play computers behind their closed doors.
Most take a bite out of life, but never get to the core.
We each have to battle our own secret war.
There are way too many sightings of blood, death and gore.
Isn't it strange? Isn't it true?
All this behavior has exhausted you!

Everybody's schedule is jam-packed and full.
They can't find time to call an old friend.
So many can't sleep well, too few take a rest.
They now take their devices wherever they go.
When is enough way too late?
Isn't it strange? Isn't it true?
All this behavior has caused a more stressed out you!

Check out the family dinner table, there's more missing than there.
With so much more available, you'd think there'd be more to share.
A better way to spend your time would be to search for someone who'll care.
You should really look inside that face in the mirror, most just primp or stare.

Everybody's running someplace, but they don't know exactly where.
The state of tranquility is so allusive and rare.
Isn't it strange? Isn't it true? All this behavior hasn't made a kinder you!

You chase after money you can't spend fast enough, you want it all yesterday.

So you give up the moment, you give away the peace.

You give most to yourself, you give in to the rat race then turn ash gray.

Some show you they love you, but you don't know how that feels, and you don't even know what to say.

You're too busy and too numb to believe there's a much better way.

Isn't it sad? Isn't it true? All this behavior has only made a lonelier you.

9600

Dust to Dawn

I think as time goes on, the kind get kinder, but the kind get fewer.
As time goes on the world gets smaller, but not closer.
The hope remains, but with less conviction.
As time goes on, machines replace and recall,
but can't reflect, replenish nor relate.
The heart and soul wants are less, but more desired.
The needs the same, but less available. . .I think.
As time goes on, the ills of society grow, the quality of life
diminishes.
But the love lingers to the end, then scatters itself over the land,
under the stars and beneath the ocean's reef.

Inside of each, one's very own private beyond.

9200

Only All of Us

What's it take to make a move?
What's it take to see another way?
What's it mean to beat the odds?
What's it mean to know but not say?

You wake up each day, while Christmas comes but once a year.
The parade passes you by, while you close your eyes and fear.

You go along singing the same old tune.
You go ahead and say something kind.
You go through mud if you have to.
You go deep inside and try to unwind.

Who's to blame if no one's at fault?
Who's to obey when there's no one to lead?
Who's to continue as the story unfolds?
Who's to suffer if no one can bleed?

You look up to pray and kneel down in thanks.
The ground inhales the sun's vast wealth.
Lightning strikes few, but at random.
You must always come to terms with yourself.

There's a lesson to be learned.
There's a friend to be hugged.
There's a mistake to be admitted.
There's a heart to be tugged.

Where can we be safe?
Why can we let go?
How can we survive?
When can we really know?

WHO'S ALL THIS ABOUT?   Only all of us.

8400

38

Pay Attention

We notice things we want to,
we notice and take note.
Some things are not recorded,
others you just let float.

How can you tell the leader, in a group of all the same?
Tiny signs might give it away.
Quickly, add up what means the most,
then go on about your day.

Do you hear the birds singing?
Can you listen and not think?
Some words are said but not understood,
but their tone will provide the missing link.

Pay attention to detail, but feel the open space,
a moment is often too long.
Crank up the music, let it rock and roll,
you've heard it before, but it's a brand new song.

Feel the ocean; touch the sand.
Feel the hand you hold.
Let the rhythm of your senses come and go at will.
Pass along your heart's true secrets, that their meanings slowly
unfold.

Love is where you'll find forgiveness.
Love is where you'll find your light.
Love is how you'll make it through.
Love is how you'll make it right.

Love is when you'll be forever.
Love is when you'll stand beside.
Love is when you'll be at peace.
Love is why you'll never hide.

72800

To Whom and How

A lover, a forever, from a chance in hell...
You know what? You just never can tell.
You go to get this, and come back with that...
Tomorrow's encounters... about what, where at?
A father says, "See ya," to a daughter of love,
then jumps off a roof. But wait, he's not a dove!
You have enough money, but you still want more.
You think you've arrived, but you can't find the door.
A miracle can happen, but only if you believe,
not everyone is blind to the lies that you weave.
Politeness, to diminished, to barely a trace,
a dangerous flaw in this human race.
The lights go out and danger sets in,
you can't hear the scream, but you can hear the pin.
So many lonely, they accept it and hide,
and deep in the middle of their hearts they have died.

A lover, a forever, from a wisp of fate...
You know what? Most things are never too late.
You begin to give up, but you won't fall apart,
for all that is left is to go back to the start.
Nobody trusts nobody, that's just about true,
you even wonder sometimes if YOU believe you.
Come over beside me, and just hold me tight,
I want to be close and let in the light.
Cry if you want to, I'll catch all of your tears,
face all of your demons, say good-bye to your fears.
To whom and how we relate is exactly who we are,
a part of the thunder or the grain of a star?

A lover, a forever, from a long time ago,
just imagine the passion and the warmth of their glow.
Each day there's a struggle some place inside,
but there's also a window a hundred feet wide.
Love is why you'll never need to hide.
Life is infinite, always open, on parade,
marching out of place are the sun, dark, and shade.

72600

40

While You Can

Sometimes you hear, "You break it...you own it."
Sometimes it's, "What you want. . .you get it."
Or, "You think it. . .you say it."
I say, "You feel it. . .you show it."

Life is one step at a time at different speeds,
during different surroundings, with different people.

Life is liquid, solid, and changing among different kinds,
containing different elements, spreading different results.

Life is not enough or too much. . . simple and profound,
giving different signals trying different paths serving different
temptations.

Life is decisions, dilemmas, and discussions...private different
sanctuaries,
demanding different struggles, joyful different blessings.

Life is heart, spirit and will.
What you start with, what you make it, what you have now. . .
accepting different concepts, listing different priorities, for different
reasons.

Life is living in different shadows, throughout different centuries,
under different regulations.

Life by plan, chance, and invasion...interpreting different dreams,
creating different images at different levels.

Love yourself if you can. . .if you will. . .if you should.

Love within, around, and back.

Love holds different standards, and different thresholds
and different expectations.
Live now. . .live more. . .love now. . .love more. . .WHILE YOU
CAN.

72200

. . . now

You need to slow down, but the world's going faster.
You start, but you never seem to finish.
Yesterday so far away, yet tomorrow is almost right here.
We lose our balance...we catch a glimpse.
We steal a kiss... we see better inside.

You can't keep up, nor do you want to,
but can you rest and still maintain?
You settle down, but keep spinning around.
Time is recorded from the eyes of an eagle.
Circumstances determine direction.
Life is fragile... full and finite.
You want it all, but for just how long?

Flowers tug at our good nature.
We relax by doing... we love by showing.
We live by relating... we are by miracle.
We don't know "how to" sometimes,
and sometimes we "have to" anyway.

If you look hard enough sometimes you might see the other side. . .
sometimes you might even find it.
Sometimes you gotta close your eyes and drift.
Sometimes you gotta let it all out and then leave it far behind.

Casual conversation, casual encounters, casual activities. . .
attired in a tux, attached to a cell phone, around the clock, on the run.
Listen lightly... step softly.
Speak silently... act accordingly.

Crawl. Walk. Trot. Run. Surge. Jump. Fly. Float. Fall Gently. Land
safely.

Take a day off, take a week away... take a month without.
Take a year over, take a lifetime. . .now

71600

Amen

Alone, we talk to animals. We wonder what they know.
Alone, we tell ourselves the truth. We open up and bend the flow.
Alone, we reach into the night, to seek the other side.
Alone, we meet our demons, real or make believe.
We mask the face of pain and wonder if we died.

Alone, we hear from deep inside what surely must be right.
Our heart allows no other choice.
Alone, the mirror seems a bit confused.
We speak the words, but from whose voice?

Alone, we dance around our sorrows.
We weep, we remember, we try to forget.
Alone, we start and alone, we end.
Alone, we journey by the lines we set.

Alone, the sights and sounds indent us.
Alone, we shuffle the cards we're dealt.
Alone, by choice is nothing like this.
It always carries its own safety belt.

Alone, we catch and hold our breath. Alone, we hear too loudly.
Alone, an angel might happen by. Alone, we admit, but not too
proudly.
Alone, the heart can convince the head. Alone, the heart can hear.
Alone, the heart conducts the music. Alone, the heart masks the fear.

Alone, way too many, much too often, by yourself.
Alone, you can be, even with another, or with all your wealth.
Alone, above, around. Alone, lost, found.
Alone, a lot, again. Alone, why, when?

Alone, not I. Alone, they cry.
Alone, we think. Alone, we try.
Alone, we begin. Alone, we die.

ALONE ALONE ALONE ALONE LONE ONE... AMEN

7700

52503

Bob Dylan, how do you create?
The past is always way too late,
life, the miraculous state, death the universal fate.

Bill Clinton, how can you sleep?
Loose ends often burrow deep,
the greedy reap, the victims weep.

Mr. Gandhi, we've been taught, but we have not yet learned.
Each generation's lovers have yearned,
the parameters have turned, the standards have burned.

Miss America, where are your clothes?
Much of this is not what we chose,
the willing propose, the sentence froze.

Sari Steiner, how come you are so sweet?
Just one other to complete,
the lonely should meet, a satin sheet.

Dad, I still see your smile,
seven years plus is not quite a while.
Empathy. . .sympathy. . . an unmeasured mile.

A CHANCE ENCOUNTER… TO A WALK DOWN AN AISLE

52503

Passage

If the outspoken minority is listened to, believed, and followed. . .
then there is no silent majority.
Do you know the power of helping out, or is money your only
priority?
How big is your car, do you have three or four?
You'll never have enough, you'll always want more.
Who you are is what you buy, they smile and agree for a piece of your pie.
Truth, respect, and love have been offered and bought.
Morals and virtues must be practiced, not just taught.

Some art and treasured memories, already selling out,
technology transforming us and spilling us all about.
Much later on the heart will fade, and be of no concern,
books and song and dancing words will be frozen or will burn.
The toughest battle we fight is deep inside our head,
it's so easy to find peace and time when we join the others dead.

Do unto others and stay true to yourself,
you may not have a dollar but you'll have all the wealth.
Try a lot of tenderness and comfort those alone,
shape and form and color the same, but the spirit itself cannot clone.
If things are going bad, stand real still and look all around.
If you've had it much worse, you'll know that desperate sound,
of silence, of screaming, of numbness, of fear.
You listen to voices of help and of hope,
unable to explain why you can't hear.

And much later when the wind is no more,
and the sky descends upon the land,
the water will dry, the air will condense,
and all that will be is a fragment of sand.
Fame and fortune, power and control,
directed the pilgrimage to the black hole.
There's so much more to find out and so much more to do,
so train yourself to see in the dark and you'll find your passage through...

I believe!

4301

Signed, Sealed and Delivered

All wrapped up in details, all wrapped up in daily stress.
Wrapped in dollars, wrapped in demands.
Wrapped in exhaustion, wrapped in woe.
Rush, rush, rush… you need more time.
You slowly forget how to slow down.

Business as usual, not much left inside at the end of the day.
Business as usual, sweat and grind, no such thing as a peaceful sleep.
Wrapped up in insanity, wrapped in disguise.
Wrapped up in closing the sale, wrapped in closets and cars.
Crowded lanes of ice and sleet, don't dare leave your cell phone off.

You look around and everyone's got that look of too much work
and way too tired and "What am I still doing here?"
Wrapped in confusion, wrapped in seclusion, nobody else inside your
head.
Wrapped around the neon lights, wrapped around the clock.
Wrapped so tight you need another you, wrapped in a slippery knot.

You wrap your dreams in last year's news, you wrap your exits in
brick.
You listen to the sounds of worry and disbelief,
then you lash out in anger from frustration.
All wrapped up in making a buck, all wrapped up in tomorrow.
All wrapped up and your chest aches a bit,
so you unwrap for a moment, but not long enough. . .

YOUR NEXT APPOINTMENT IS AN HOUR AWAY!

Wrapped up in yourself, wrapped down to the bone.
Wrapped next to a landmine, wrapped inside a spider's web.
All wrapped up in hollow gold, all wrapped up in everything to lose.
All wrapped up ALONE.

41101

46

Eyelash

Rejection. . .dejection. . .reflection.
Biology. . .   psychology. . .ideology.
The world runs and shakes and screams. . .
we scatter and batter and shatter. . .hateful chatter. . .fear-fueled matter.

We're all just hanging on:

> On to some hope.
> On to some promise.
> On to some dream.
> On to some sanity.
> On to some dimes.

Hanging on for that moment of truth.

We're vulnerable and visible.
We're so unsure of what's next.
A secret in every family. . . a struggle in every mind.
A mirror behind every smile. . .a cloudy head atop a weary body.

Survival. . .arrival. . .revival.
Risking now for a better tomorrow.
Choosing love, awaiting sorrow.
Attitude. . .latitude. . .gratitude.

The world stumbles, then crumbles, then humbles.
We finally see the light. . .but it is past us.
We finally stop the fight. . .we are but a few. . .left.
We finally sleep at night. . .but we sleep alone.
We finally end our plight. . .but our time was just a moment.
We finally know what's right. . .but why did it take so long?

From here to there. . .from when to where.
From earth to air. . .from always to rare.
From blasphemy to prayer.

We're all just hanging on:
By our imagination. . . By our fear. . . By our instincts. . .
By our will. . .By our love…

BY AN EYELASH

53103

47

At the Masquerade Ball

Deliriously exhausted:
the struggles the pace the killings the money the distance between
heartaches and headaches, failures and frailties, fears and foes.
Working longer and harder for less,
losing jobs and dignity for more.

Repeatedly disappointed:
the promises the heroes. . .ho, ho
the priorities the excuses the justice. . .oh, no.
We dream we wish we hope we quit we lose we crumble.
Drama pushed to disaster.
Humor with a jagged edge.
Sadness in the masses.
Morality in a see-through blouse… at the masquerade ball.

We lie to ourselves, as we twist the truth.
We pretend to care for some reward.
We pray with a bleeding heart.
We exist without living.
We live without loving. . .as many as we could.
                    As ourselves we should.
                    By others if we would.
 Before and after all this. . .serenity.

61203

Spring

Birth/Hope

More Than Maybe

Maybe a few blank pages will speak a thousand words,
maybe silence sounds louder than stampeding buffalo herds.
"I don't know, I'm not sure, I'm too afraid to say."
Maybe if I don't respond, the question will fade away.

You can plead the Fifth Amendment, you can pretend you didn't hear.
Maybe if you close your eyes, you can catch each falling tear.
Choice, our sacred freedom, love lost our deepest pain,
maybe if we care enough, we'll create an endless chain.

Not all are free nor equal, under the red, white and blue,
maybe if we really listen, we'll understand a different view.
Will and perseverance combine both heart and mind,
maybe if you be yourself, some peace and calm you'll find.

Maybe when we express ourselves, we should follow them with deeds.
Maybe someday we'll narrow the gap… between our wants and our needs.

60403

Dismissed

Before:
Begin, pause, stop, restart, fast-forward, pause, stop... end.
Whatever, you can't understand... at all.
You can't comprehend... the fall.
You can't fathom... the thought.
You can't conceive... getting caught.

Fast forward twenty years:
You can't believe... now you.
You can't imagine... how true.
You now allow... the pain.
You now splatter... like rain.
You now descend... all alone.
You now slouch... when prone.
You now hide... deep inside.
You now forsake... any pride.

Fast forward just one year, or so:
You understand forgiveness... right now.
You understand consequences... but how?
You understand distance... family first.
You understand love... hollow thirst.
You understand humanity... selfish lot.
You understand eternity... vintage plot.

Fast forward to today:
I want to call... no one there.
I want to pretend... then double dare.
I want to sob... one fallen tear.
I want to confess... then wipe clear.
I want to manipulate reality... instead of blaming fate.
I want to say goodbye... but I'm too late.

Fast forward, fast rewind, fast forward way too fast:
Nobody can beat time… nobody can last.
You don't know about tomorrow…you can't bring back the past.

Fast forward, hold on tight, fast forward, embrace the night.
Fast forward, twist and turn:
Once again, suffer and learn… light the fire, and help it burn.

Fast forward, to this finality:
Sometimes life is found beneath a crack,
I want my long time, dear friend back.
You will not be dismissed, as a friend, as a son, as a brother, or a dad.

This is all way, way, too sad.

62801

A New Purpose

We're fragmented souls... lost in focus, lost in disbelief, lost in horror.
We're fragmented souls... unsure, unaccustomed, at times,
unavailable... Undeniably so.
Scattered thoughts... random actions... sacred hearts.
Now, new devices... new techniques... new moralities.

People alone... in fact or emotion.
People alone... at midnight or dawn.
People alone... by loss or intent.

Our whole... sometimes half.
Our body moves... but not its shadow.
Our body weeps... but only the eyes respond.
Our body trembles... our spirit holds us together.

We're fragmented souls...not in purpose, but in trust,
not in resolve, but in revenge, not in faith, but in conscience.
We're fragmented souls where...fear replaces caution,
empathy replaces sympathy, nightmare replaces daydream,
Unity replaces factions.
LIFE IS SO DIFFERENT.
There's a new dimension, with a renewed direction,
a new energy, with a renewed fury, a new challenge, with a renewed
alliance.

COME FORTH... all the kind.
COME FORTH... all the able.
COME FORTH... all the tribes.
COME FORTH... all the LEADERS.

COME FORTH... to defend.
COME FORTH... to preserve.
COME FORTH... to unite.
COME FORTH... to SURVIVE.

RETURN... to freedom.
RETURN... to grace.
RETURN... to peace.
RETURN... to LOVE.

92201

53

Deception

The spider's web… what a piece of art.
Come close, and behold my beauty.
Come close, and touch my lace.
It's spread across and down my body… and up my face.

Welcome to temptation.
Welcome to erotic delights.
Find yourself a place to rest…
Perhaps we'll invite another guest.

Only in a certain light will I become exposed.
I hardly move.
I hardly am.
I hardly make a sound.

My lines run true, they circle and stretch…
There are no "no trespass" signs.
LIPSTICK RED, BEDROOM EYES, AN ISLAND HOME ATOP
A HILL.
"Come close. Come here. No need to stay away."
"Come watch me spin… come watch me sway."

A THUNDERBOLT, A SHOOTING STAR,
A RAINBOW ACROSS THE SKY.
A builder, a creator, a sculptor… a poet of space and design.
You'll let down all your inhibitions. You'll put away all your fears.
Your capture will be swift, yet silent. You'll surrender…then be mine.

So, just relax, let yourself go.
Escape? Not likely… so don't even try.
Because, here with me, you'll be at peace,
when your time has come to die.

91202

Light Grey

The years are burning away.
The tears are all dried up.
The cheers are scattered... at best.

NO TIME TO DUST OUR FEATHERS OFF.

Bend backwards, as far as you can go,
the mirrors reveal the truth...
our peers are not surprised by much,
our gears need some repair.

Our souls have searched and found.
Our goals... now tempered by time.
Our roles include reverse.

CATCH YOUR BREATH, THEN STEP BACK IN.

A few more funerals.
A few more pills.
More aids to relieve our aches.

More signs to heed.
More victims to bleed.
More love we need.

Our town is now global... a forty-eight hour day.
Main street behind us, the sidewalk ahead.
Even in confusion, even in despair, even at the very end...
The heart must lead the way.

92802

Keep In Touch

No fanfare, no parade, no spotlights on the moon,
No long goodbyes, no filtered kiss...
Some things are never too soon.

No reason why, no dessert, no leaves left on the tree,
No jokes to laugh, no lame excuse...
Story-telling on Grandpa's knee.

Keep in mind, keep in heart, keep in distance...
KEEP IN TOUCH.

A lost number, a stubborn cause, or just a memory lapse?
A safety check, a revelation, a word of praise, perhaps?
A follow up, a long overdue return, a chance to make amends.
Take a day, take the time to reach out to your friends.

Keep in hope, keep in song, keep in truth...
KEEP IN TOUCH.

Rush hour, rush minute, rush until you drop.
Rush into, rush from, rush until you POP!
A faster meal, a faster deal...
you'd better slow down your pace and feel.

Keep in shape, keep in prayer, keep in spirit...
KEEP IN TOUCH.

Stay part of the others, stay close to the mothers,
stay connected... in honor and deed.
Stay tuned to the children, stay aware of the strangers,
stay loving... it's all that we need.
Forgiveness our challenge... kindness our creed.

121102

30 x 2

Forever is right now.

Turn it on, turn it up, turn it over.
Twist it, twirl it, try it.
Turn it different.
Turn it right, left, turn it around.
Turn it in, turn it out.
Turn it with truth, with deed... with love.

Forever is right now.

First... years.
Then months,
then weeks,
then days,
then hours,
then minutes.
Now... moments.

Forever is right now.

111204

Just

Just a blink.
Just a pause.
Just a glance.
Just a murmur.
Just a speck.
Just a touch.
Just a hint.
Just a taste.
Just life…just all.

82803

Symptoms

Smiles far and few between.
Hiding eyes in fear of being seen.
Survival kits and weapons bought like chewing gum.
No more "just a few," now a swelling amount of some.
The so-called "silent majority" sleep with buzzing in their heads.
A thousand homeless people with a million unused beds.
Symptoms.

Songs of woe and disbelief, of broken hearts and shattered dreams.
Fallen idols and anti-heroes, not much is what it seems.
Newspaper headlines and by-lines scream of violence and gloom.
Closets full of secrets, silence fills the room.
Symptoms.

All the faces, fearful and worn…innocence lost too soon after being born.
Rings and things neon lit, pieces of hope that never fit.
Hate and greed twist round and round,
fire and freedom beneath the ground.
Symptoms… conditions… up in arms against our will.

Symptoms… finality… the world now still.

92003

Biding My Time

Waiting on a rainbow.
Waiting for the meltdown.
Waiting on a phone call.
Waiting for an even flow.
Biding my time.

Waiting for the sun.
Waiting for the next kiss.
Waiting on a promise.
Waiting to be undone.
Biding my time.

Waiting for a dream come true.
Waiting to forgive.
Waiting on a rainbow.
Waiting by you.
Biding my time

Waiting by those in need.
Waiting for a peaceful world.
Waiting in a safety net.
Waiting for the truth to lead.
Biding my time.

Making a statement.
Taking a chance.
Exhausting all options, rhythm, and rhyme.
Loving and loved.
Biding my time.

11803

PC TV VCR VHS DVD

Language adaptation, micro-contraption.
Pills to rid ills.
Pills to stop kills.
Pills to breathe, pills to sleep, pills to prevent, pills to invent.
Pills to stay thin, pills to help win, pills to fuck, pills to sustain.
Pills to unnerve, pills to relax, pills to relieve.
Pills to warm chills, pills to climb hills, and pills to detain wills.

Fast is not fast enough.
Slow and easy. . .when?
Race, rush, "Run Lola Run."
E-mail, FedEx, speed dial and fax.
Buy a rocket ride to the moon.
Buy some pleasure. . .use it soon.
Midnight's twisted sister. . .high noon.

I miss my Dad.
I miss Larry and Lowell.
I miss the quiet, the sun, the innocence of youth.
I miss playing baseball, playing football…
I miss the energy of youth.
I miss my family and friends who live far away.
I miss the desert, the pool, the mountains so bold.
I miss the resilience of youth.

But…
I don't spend much time missing.
I'd rather spend that time kissing.
I don't spend much time in the past.
I live right now trying always to slow down the fast.
I don't think long term, the future is today. . .
so live your life, harmless to others, but live it your way.

4102

So be it. . .

Love is most definitely the little things. . .so is life.
YOU are all of my heart. . .so it is.
Love feels great, both giving and taking. . .so do more.
Turn the corner, round the bend. . .so now what?
Look at the face, look in the eyes, there shouldn't be much surprise. . .
so do it!
Over time, the truth will rear its transparent head. . .so it shall.
The whispers of intimacy, the roars of the heart. . .so be bold.
The moments, the tokens, the sidewalks, the in-betweens. . .so be
there.
The mind can invent pleasures, stay distant, magnify fears...so be
aware.
There is no pretend in love, nor is there apathy, abuse or deceit...so
WE know.
Life is a bunch of lines.
Time is a bunch of promises.
Death is a bunch of maybes. . .so be it.

2103

Plants and Beasts

It's not what you leave behind, it's what you give right now.
You can change the future right now,
you can say something, do something, build something, discover
something.
You can fuck up, fuck off, fuck this or that.
You can scream or say nothing at all.

It's not what you do for a living, it's how you do it.
You can tremble in fear, you can close your eyes and be safe.
You can look in the mirror and see your reflection.
You can look deep inside for the truth.

It's not what money can buy or which God or who wins,
it's what love can overcome, and which path soothes your soul, and
who tries.
You can be down and out, you can be born into poverty or shame.
You can be confined each day of your life.
You can run with the pack, you can walk all alone.
You can pretend to be happy, you can pretend to be someone else.
You can run, jump and dance.
You can touch, hug and kiss.
You can mend your own heart over time.

It's not what life wants out of you, it's what you want out of life.
It's not the photos in the scrapbook, it's the moments in between.
You can wish and pray and dream and hope.
You can be grateful or bitter or both.
You can say what you feel and do what you say.
You can clearly know we're all one.

2303

Gulp

Life's about trying and crying and sighing, and denying and flying and dying.
Life's about giving and living, sons that don't call their dads.
Brothers, now strangers, cross paths and say hello,
but share only their early years as lads.
The young treating the old with indifference and disrespect.
Heroes not concerned about their cause, nor their effect.

The greed associated with dollars makes no sense.
The trust we want, but don't give, anchors our self-imposed barbed wire fence.
We're running out of tune, out of whack, out of time,
victims turned inside out, while perpetrators hardly ever pay for their crime.

Life is about hoping and coping, about bending and lending,
about missing and kissing, about clashing and dashing.
Life is about dancing and romancing, about turning and learning and burning.
Life is a roll of the dice, some win, many pay the price.
Life is about you and me and all of us and all of the others,
about sharing and daring and caring.
Life is love, hate, peace and war. . .a yield sign, a beware warning, an open door,
about good times and bad, joyful, quiet and sad,
about right now, with an eye on the future and a mirror on the past.

Walk near the water. Walk under the moon.
Walk into the stillness. Walk very far, very soon.
LIFE, try a sip, take a drink, inhale, indulge… GULP

62401

Segments

A vision and a dance,
a song inside romance.
You stand in line and you take a chance.
THE ROAD IS NEVER CLEAR.

A laugh a giggle a joke or two, some pain may be put on hold.
To get somewhere and find yourself, you must gather in and then unfold.
A heart of precious gold.
CHANGE IS ALWAYS NEAR.

Your dreams are real, right then and there,
a smile you can gladly share.
Imagine yourself all alone, but only if you dare.
A SCREAM YOU'LL ALWAYS HEAR.

The words are the same, with just a few things out of place.
Then there's that entitlement thing, about part of the human race.
It is the capture, it's not the chase.
HIDE AWAY YOUR GREATEST FEAR.

As the years go by, you lose more friends.
Life is about how you live it, not how it ends.
There's going to be a breaking point, after way too many bends.
YOU CAN HIDE BEHIND A SMILE, BUT NOT BEHIND A TEAR.

Always open a time you come and go.
Love is all you really need to endure and to grow.
Only if you look up at the stars can you ever see them glow.

TAKE A LONG HARD LOOK AT THE FACE IN THE MIRROR.

Pigments, environments, segments,
I love you at least all of the time. . .always upon a time.

7301

Off the Edge

We're all racing on the edge:
on the edge of a prayer
on the edge of a promise
on the edge of morality
on the edge of tomorrow
on the edge of war
on the edge of sanity.

We're all just hanging on to the notion of equality:
to the whims of fate
to the scales of justice
to the shadows of truth
to the other side. . .hanging on to the edge.

The eggs are broken, the feathers ruffled, the glass about to burst.
The air is full of smoke, the candle almost dim.
The hardships many, the dollars few.
Some connections break apart. . .the edge is wall to wall dripping in
blood.
Nature's on the edge of futility.
Humanity on the edge of extinction.
Love on the edge of trust.
Passion on the edge of peace.

DEATH. . . OFF THE EDGE OF LIFE

3903

The First and Only

History's relentless march through today, on to tomorrow,
lines of curves and motion, circles and arrows, and bloodied paths
and allies.
We tilt and we spin and we take midnight by surprise.
We camouflage and we hide and we search outside and alone.
We are infinite and infant, we are dust and pods, we are fragments of
air.
Time blinks and stares and stretches and blinds; it looks away with no
remorse.
Light and dark become one, peace before and after.
The rain to snow to ice then melts, then burns, then again and again.

We disguise and discover, we evolve and evaporate.
We use science to advance and spirit to survive.
A bolt of lightning precedes a thunderous roar.
We gasp and sigh and whisper secrets and promises,
and we pretend and imagine and wonder and weep .
Next to the closet, upon the basement floor, around the world and
back,
introductions are made, relationships formed.
Love and fear embrace in passion, pride and will.

SAVE THE FIRST DANCE FOR ME

We measure and compare and we push ourselves
to become one and the same with machines.
Tick tock, ha-ha, tick tock, boohoo, tick tock, tick tock, your time is
up.
Goodbye, hello, and round and round we go.
Too soon, too late, too gosh-darn bad.
Too much, too fast, too gosh-darn sad.
Too close, too middle, too far, you lost, you found, you are.
Tulips and rainbows and dawn and slivers of moon.

SAVE THE FIRST DANCE FOR ME.

72701

67

Etch-a-Sketch

Temptation's colorful gown of light yellows
and deep reds and purples and brushed silver and glitter.
Strands of whites and browns then blues and greens.

Temptation's very thin lace disguise.
Subtleties and absurdities evoke, provoke and entice at every turn...
just next door, up the road, one after another and ever after.

Temptation's longevity and confidence.
Time is always on its side...just one time, just one more time,
just once, I promise, just once I dare.
You can't have it, so you want it. You can't do it, so you show them.

Temptation: it dangles and whispers it sways and peeks.
It stares and reveals, it dazzles, screams, and thrusts.
Camouflaged and choreographed, it rewards, perhaps many.
It punishes, perhaps but one.

A question that demands an answer. . .
AT WHAT SACRIFICE?

8301

The Sun's Downtime

The night…
fear attired in tuxedo black.
Listen closely, if you dare…
the spiders mate,
the predators wait.
The night.

Around the corner,
inside your house.
Just a heartbreak away…
the fire burns,
the Jesus turns.
The night.

Letting go
of the long, hard day.
Romance dancing
under soft neon glow.
Sweet smiles persuade…
as candles fade.
The night.

Peace settles in,
almost too late.
A star… a moon… a dream.
Huddled close, the lovers drift…
silence, nighttime's gift.
The night.

Mystery prevails.
Secrets told.
Intimacy exposed.
Prayers recited.
Memories haunt…silhouettes gaunt.
The night.

Quiet awakens.
Giants tiptoe.
Heartbeats flutter.
Parties razzle...jesters dazzle.
The night...

an unborn child before its light.

42399

Summer

Imagination/Passion

Identification

Imagine, create, envision.
Formless, unconscious, natural passion, poetry, perspective.
Invention. . .experience growth.
Change. . .interpretation, attitude.
From deep inside, a language of its own.
A new adventure, a variable of time and place and circumstance.
Emotional expressions, evocative exclamation. . .a reflection of you.

Parallels and comparatives. . .identification.
A journey of discovery and re-examination and perhaps conclusion.
A declaration of fact and delusion.
A reality of "right this moment."
A clarity of "who you are and what you feel."

Minutes later, a reminder.
Weeks later, a reference.
Months later, a memory.
Years later, a mystery.
Forever a confession.

8401

Time's Shadow

Are you happy without the edge and discomfort of intrusion?
Do you live the good life or is that a delusion?
Is locked into place your endless conclusion?
Will you wake up with the dawn or evaporate in seclusion?
Your terms, your choice, your truth.
Time blinks and years go by,
your birth, your life, your death.
Time clones itself but with imperfections,
your luck, your wish, your fate.
Time reveals its secrets and masks,
your hate, your indifference, your love.

Have you betrayed yourself, thus guilty of treason?
Will protecting your heart be a good enough reason?
Can you survive and progress from season to season?
Your humanities, your relationships, yourself.
TIME'S SHADOW: OUR HAUNTING COMPANION.

8801

73

The End

Racing, chasing, facing tomorrow, today.
Pushing too fast, too hard, too much. Look out!
Road rage, neon cage, blood on the page.
One working two, just to keep even. Look about!
Blame society, blame heritage, blame another. Look, then hide!
The heart fails, the spirit smolders, the will concedes. Look inside!

Nice people doing some not nice things.
Greed and necessity stab you in the back.
"No mercy," shout the king and all the king's men.
"No mercy," shout the common folk.
Random killings, random brutalities, random victims…
a million random tears.
One fucked up place, one fucked up race.
Pockets of safety here and there, lockets of love, drops of care.

You're thirteen at seven, twenty-one at twelve.
Speed, a requirement, not a choice.
Fear, a silence, not a voice.
"Be you," an anthem.
"Be free," a blessing or pursuit.
"Be me," a plea for understanding.
Be together, yourself and another.
Be easy, so you can still be.

Do what you can, then do some more,
then band together for strength and survival.
It's the only way out of this vicious "leave no witness" spiral
of metal and wires and ashes
heading much too quickly to
THE END!!!

81101

A Conversation

You don't have to conform, you don't have to apologize.
You don't have to be a prisoner, nor wear a disguise.
No more bullshit and no more lies,
Life is a series of laughter and cries.

We know so much more, now that we've made it this far,
We know so much more from the pain.
We let go of parts so that we can remain.
We let go of the past so that we can stay sane.
Give fear a jolt because you've got nothing to lose,
and so much to gain.

If this doesn't work, something else will, two steps backwards,
one leap ahead.
It's only what you do, not necessarily what you said.
You just need to trust your heart, and utilize your head.

Sacrifice and apprehension are constants at every turn.
At every new experience, there'll be something different you can
learn.
How you make your mark in life is only your concern.

81901

75

Tune

Listen very closely to the sounds outside your voice.
Digest the information, then react and make a choice.
Pay attention to the noise that moves you up or down.
Does the city make you feel alive,
or is contentment a small rural town?

Talk less and hear much more,
add new dimensions to your inner core
Speak your mind and show your heart.
Reduce pollution. Do your part!

82501

It's All About Time

It's been a long time since I ran the bases.
It's been a long time since I've seen some faces.
It's been a long time since I've had no worries.
It's been a long time indeed.

It's been a long time since I started school.
It's been a long time since the golden rule.
It's been a long time since innocence.
It's been a long time indeed.

It's been a short time since I've laughed and cried.
It's been a short time since I chanced and tried.
It's been a short time since discovery.
It's been a short time indeed.

It's been a short time since I've witnessed a dove.
It's been a short time since I've kissed and made love.
It's been a short time since goodbye.
It's been a short time indeed.

It's been no time since the dawn brought today.
It's been no time since my dad passed away.
It's been no time since Larry and Lowell, as well.
It's been no time since I've stumbled and fell.
It's been no time indeed.

It's been no time since time was true.
It's been no time since there was you.
It's been no time since change.
It's been no time indeed.

You're my white shining,
my red simmering,
my blue stretching.
You're my silver lining.

82901

The Eagles

Each song, a poem.
Each poem, a story.
Each story, a life.
Each life, a journey.
Each journey, a lesson.
Each lesson, a discovery.
Each discovery, a beginning.
Each beginning, a creation.
Each creation, a miracle.
Each miracle, a song.
Each song, a poem.

And on and on and on.
We march, step by step, one by one.
Time, our companion.
Change, our constant.
Space, our provider.
Love, our savior.

83101

From Here To There

Golden leaves, golden years...life is a busy signal, don't you know?
Gold into amber into clear,
opaque into linen into sheer.
Much to enjoy...too much to fear,
something new, something old is always quite near.

Life is a busy signal, ain't it so?
You work and play and rest,
you think you've arrived, but you're always taking some test.
Red into pink into flesh,
you aim up above, then you lower your sight.
Golden years, golden tears.

Life is a busy signal, won't let go.
Fast, faster, not fast enough...we're all in a timeless race.
A cosmic pace.
A breakdown chase.
A Picasso face.
A ghostly trace.

The only sanctuary deep inside,
from yourself, you cannot hide.
Black into black into black,
forward march, there's no turning back.
Golden leaves, golden light...the dawn before the night.

Life is a busy signal, can't it flow?
Can't speak the language, can't do it all,
can't keep it simple, can't climb each wall.
Can't have the pleasure without some pain,
can't give up or you'll go insane.

White into white into white,
the golden ride on an endless flight.
Life is a busy signal, doesn't it show?
Life is a busy signal, Ho-Ho-Ho.
Ho-hum-oh!

102501

Happy Birthday To Me!

56 just strolled into 57,
wasn't I 45 just a few years ago?
57 and counting...how many will it be?
I've been blissfully high and hopelessly low.

56 just strolled into 57,
with bumps and bruises, with glasses and gray.
57 and thinking about me and the world,
I've gone 'round and 'round, then tried a new way.

56 just strolled into 57,
a bit wiser now, but not all the time.
57 and rocking, still air-guitaring those tunes,
I've thrown away those dollars and saved not a dime.

56 just strolled into 57,
some friends and my dad are gone, but right here.
57 and hoping, peaceful existence for all man-kind,
I've been in the clouds and been crystal clear.

56 just strolled into 57,
I'm now more cautious and forgetful, more able and aware.
57 and knowing how time must not pass you by,
I try by myself, but it's far better to share.

56 just strolled into 57,
beauty lies within, all around, you don't have to look hard.
57 and grateful for you and many to love,
I've discovered myself when I let down my guard.

56 just strolled into 57,
life's been good, life's been hard, life's been wavy, life's been fast.

57 and wondering...is this all there is?
I've opened my heart and lived by it's beat, and this legacy is the
shadow I cast.

111101/111201

Cobwebs

Instead of places, now just some empty spaces, and a few minor traces.
Now, just some random sketches and a few vague recollections, instead of faces.
Clarity behind glasses, hearing devices, magnifiers and mirrors.
As the years wear on, we're not just falling apart,
we're replacing and replenishing, re-thinking and re-scheduling.

We're now in a slow-down mode...our minds, our bodies, our movements.
As the years wear on, cobwebs hold captive our memories.
Past truths become conjecture, events fuzzy, situations confusing.
Pills, morning, noon and night...wrinkles, no cream can disguise.
All this and more as the years wear on.
All this and more, so what's the point?

Here it is. It's as simple as this.
No, these later years are not golden,
and no, these later years are not easy.
But...
The mind has a will and the body has a reserve
and love has a way of mending and healing and providing and caring.

These later years have a sense of history and understanding of life,
a respect of time and an appreciation of right now.
No waiting...no pauses...no in-betweens
as the years wear on, as the years wear thin.

Love...our constant companion, our strength and our peace.

12501

At Your Leisure

Everybody, just about, has been going through some rough times.
Necessity dollars...recreational dimes.
Run, run, run, run, run, run, run.
Is anyone able to peek at the sun?
Is anyone rested when the day is done?
Can you stretch out your mind and really have fun?
Will you keep what's important or end up with none?
Run, run, run, run, run, run, run.

Everybody, just about, has been feeling unsafe, feeling nothing's real
clear.
Instant recall... forever tears.
Run, run, run, run, run, run, rest.
Do you always have to be the best? Is this all there is or is it just a
test?
Have you started yet on your spiritual quest?
Are you at home in your body or are you a guest?
Run, run, run, run, run, run, rest.

Everybody, just about, has been putting aside daily contact
with family and friends.
Sweet whispers... nobody sends.
Run, run, run, run, run, run, stop.
In the big picture, is there someplace to crop?
How much will you give up to reach the very top?
Can you get back up even after you flop?
Do you actually hear the noise right before you drop?
Run, run, run, run, run, run, stop.

Everybody, just about, has been hoping things will change.
Old priorities...must re-arrange.
Run, run, run, run, run, run, die.

Aren't you sorry you didn't even try?
Were you able to see them all say their last good bye?
Was your last breath a peaceful sigh?
Not much quality, but you know why.
Run, run, run, run, run, run, die.

Everybody, just about, has been down, if not out.
Ghostly heart... no doubt!

1902

Peanut Butter & Jelly

The inner sanctum of the outer limits.
The profound moments of the infinite minutes.

The harsh consequences of the promised land.
The fossilized truths of the ocean's sand.

The painful lessons of failure and strife.
The cloudy journeys of love and life.

2402

A Beatle Reminder

So many close are so far away,
tomorrow and yesterday are just thoughts of today.
You sleep on and off, if you sleep at all,
We think we're so big, but we're really so small.

Once in a while, everything goes your way,
they have what you want and they hear what you say.
Then there are times that drag you down and around,
they torture and puncture without any sound.

Can you stop yourself from dwelling on the shit?
Can you take your worries out of your head
and find someplace else for them to fit?
Life is a series of yeses and noes.
Life is a journey of lilacs and woes.

It's always up to only you to change the way you live.
When you understand that love is all that you need,
you'll get much more than what you give.

92400

John Lennon

I wonder about tomorrow's youth...
I wonder if any would deliver the truth.
I wonder if death is just a rebirth into a different form...
I wonder if fear will remain the norm.
I wonder if peace will ever come...
I wonder when the good will be only the some.
I wonder about the heavens above...
I wonder about all the people I love.
I wonder about what other beings know...
I wonder if the stars will always glow.
I wonder about the choices we make...
I wonder about the principles we forsake.

I wonder what's far beneath the mighty ocean's floor...
I wonder if a battered ego can find the strength to soar.
I wonder when the apple is bitten just what poison will fill its core.
I wonder, in the future, will there be a welcome mat in front of anybody's door.
I wonder how people find some hope when all they have known is war.
But, most of all, I wonder if the day will come
when love is abundant and hate is no more.

Let us "Imagine."

51302

Corners

Incidents and accidents, struggles to get past,
lessons from the daily grind, just what truth do they cast?
Jungle cats kill for food, they have no other choice.
The expression of pain in all of us has but one unmistakable voice.
Turning points and take off points and points of no return.
Take a chance, make that move, you've got so much more to learn.
At some point in time, something will happen
that will forever change your plight.
It may be by chance it may be by intent,
it may even be the darkest dark before the brightest light.

Did you develop a tumor, did you go broke once and for all?
Did a loved one suddenly die, did you, yourself, hear an angel call?
Did you search and search and search some more to discover the real
you?
Do you really like who you are?
How deep is the wound,
How swollen is the scar?

Have you met someone who happened by,
did you look them right in the eye?
Were you able to listen, to understand,
were you able to open wide and feel safe to cry?

If you had yesterday back would you change it?
Would you squeeze more out of it?
Would you just leave it alone right where it is...way far behind?
Do you pray there's an ever-after?
Do you hope tomorrow will come?

Don't wait for an intervention. Don't wait until your passion just whispers.
Don't wait for a knock on the door.
Find your spark and if it's in your heart, you don't have to search anymore.

Take out all the color everything is black or white.
Take out all the issues everything is wrong or right.
Take out all the minutes everything is day or night.
Take out all the pressure everything is loose or tight.

Love is the warmth. Love is the smile. Love is the constant. Love is the light.

42902

Link

Way too many lifestyle pills,
way too many executed wills.
Way too many unpaid bills,
way too many steep hills.
SPEED kills.

One does the job that two did before,
now all that's important is the final score.
Red into green, down to the core,
you can't feel safe behind a plastic door.
DANGEROUS floor.

Way too many nervous years,
way too many left behind fears.
Way too many dusty mirrors,
way too many lonely tears.
WHISPERED cheers.

You can't avoid the rat race,
you can't escape the constant chase.
Tired eyes on a tired face,
not much kindness, hugs or grace.
UNFORGIVING pace.

Down the way an Indian head penny...the only trace.

41802

The art of imagination.
The will of concentration.
The breath of emancipation.
The spark of fascination.
The lure of intoxication.
The silence of relaxation.
The nerves of anticipation.
The smiles of recreation.
The safety of affirmation.
The effort of participation.
The esteem of satisfaction.
The mystery of creation.
The muscle of exclamation.
The spirit of dedication.
The thought of vacation.
The courage of transformation.
The pulse of elation.
The morals of integration.
The wisdom of interpretation.
The discoveries of education.
The architects of transportation.
The footprints of migration.
The accomplishments of cooperation.

LOVE OF SELF

41302

Please

Can't watch the news. Can't stop the war.
Can't stop the tears. How many more?
Can't see their faces. Can't count the dead.
Can't rewind time. All blood is red!

Can't understand. Can't sleep at night.
Can't let it go. Shine right now immaculate light.
Can't give up hope. Can't forget the brave.
Can't disguise my heart. Love we must save.

Stop the killing. Stop the horror.
Stop the ignorance. Stop the insanity.
Stop the lies. Stop the torture.
Stop the caskets and martyrs. Stop the bombs and mayhem.

STOP! PLEASE STOP!

Stop the injustice. Stop the hate.
It's very nearly way too late!

41302

Me, Myself, and I

A casual encounter stirred up a dormant sense.
A neighbor down the street put up a barbed wire fence.
The sky grew dark by late afternoon.
The church piano played out of tune.

The robins turned into black, black crows,
their joyful sounds became awful woes.
The cemetery's ground began to shake.
A priceless gem turned out a fake.

By dinner time the town was still.
The summer's heat began to chill.
A ghost appeared inside my head.
The words I heard were never said.

The thunder roared, the lightning flashed.
The marmalade pie turned into ash.
My eyes rolled back, my mouth went dry.
I could not move. I could not try.

An ancient face stared down at me.
The woman's face became a he.
I stepped out of line, but stayed in place.
I looked away, but still saw his face.

The clock struck 12, I screamed, "No more!"
He stayed right there, and locked the door.
My strength gave out. My mind gave way
to years ago, to that awful day...
when I gave up hope and broke apart,
when all that was left was a trembling heart.

I swallowed hard. I looked straight ahead.
I made quite sure I wasn't dead.
I caught my demon with a surprise left hook.
I held him down and made him look.
He understood me now. He felt my intent.
His image faded, my message sent.
The grass now green, time slowed down.
Couples dressed to party downtown.
The sun came up, the children sang.
I straightened up, the doorbell rang.
That casual encounter walked right in.
I asked at last, "Where have you been?"

"Behind the moon, underneath a rock."
I awoke last night. I heard a knock.
"My mistake," he said. Then disappeared.
I knew right then… it was only ME I feared.

62099

Inspiration

You've been sketched a thousand times…
Colored, painted, photographed, filmed, sculpted.
With wings, with child, with passion, dance, and wild abandon.
With clothes, without… vulnerable, desirable.
With strength and courage…   with lust and love.
With purpose, need, and sacrifice.
Arms open… arms around… arms holding on tight.

A thousand times over you've been adored.
Beauty in flesh, sturdy in heart,
curves and form… texture and tone.

Your spirit surrounds us all…your devotion keeps us warm.
Your resolve keeps us steady…your body gives us life.
Your will gives us hope…your wisdom gives us direction.
Your love gives us safety,
Spring flowers and Summer breezes…
Autumn colors and Winter reflections.

You are… need and want, fire and water,
mother and child, friend and lover.
You are… the moon's glow,
 the sun's shine, the stars' sparkle.

You keep us one… you keep us calm,
a whisper, a song, a poem, a prayer.
A thousand times over you've been named,
but time and place have not changed you.

You are history's shadow… and tomorrow's footprints.
You are peace… you are forgiveness…you are grace.
A smile and welcome gently line your face…a lady gowned in Angel's
lace.
You are woman.

21801 Paris, France

94

The Fifth Season

Homage

Taps

The silent echo of taps…

Stand up, stand straight, stand with respect and prayer.
Those before us, mostly young,
their lives sacrificed, freedom their cause.
This nation's bravest souls, forever in our hearts.

The chilling beauty of taps…

Not to remind us, but to engage us, to challenge us, to envelop us.
Seek peace, but protect democracy.
"Do unto others," but, be true to thyself.
Promote education, cooperation, kindness and equal opportunity.

The inherent sadness of taps…

Our dead, their families, the casualties of war.
The victims of war. The ghosts of war.
Numbers on the pages, names on the wall.
Faces in the photos, bones in the ground.
Watch them salute, watch them march.
Watch their eyes as they remember the screams of pain,
the blood outside, the sounds of gunfire, the smell of death.

The universal suffering of taps…

Take a moment, take an hour, take a day, week, or two,
to honor the thousands of soldiers black and white, young and old,
men and women, rich and poor,
who took their turn in line, their place in time, their belief in
obligation.
Give a dollar, give a hundred, give as much as you can
to those survivors now restrained and confined and disfigured and
tormented by the horrors and tragedies of combat.

The haunting grace of taps...

On this November day, just slightly different from the rest,
we count our blessings through their eyes.
We choose and endure and prosper through their courage
We accept and befriend and protect and love through their hearts.
We continue on through their sacrifice.

The timeless rendering of taps...

Today I celebrate my birthday in your honor,
with respect and gratitude and sorrow
and a diminishing, yet constant ray of hope.

111202

Every Day

Dear Dad: I sure miss you. You know it's Father's Day real soon.
I miss your smile, your warmth, your strength, your love.
I miss the calmness of your ways.
This is my Father's day card for you.
Just over five years, you remain deep in my heart,
and all of your loved ones feel the same.
Honor and truth stand behind your name.
Thanks for the lessons, thanks for the voice.
Thanks for the patience, thanks for the choice.
I miss our talks, I miss your song.
I miss our hugs, I miss your forgiveness when I do wrong.

Dear Dad: Happy Father's Day.
I love you so much… I wish I could see you, I wish we could touch.
When I look at my kids, I see you in them.
When I look at Mom, I see you in love.
When I look in the mirror, I feel you inside.
When I look at the world, I don't have to hide.
I'm glad some of you rubbed off on me.
I hope you're someplace where you are safe and you are free.

Fair man, nice man, good man, family man.
Provider, teacher, friend and dad.
You're the very best father I could ever have had.
And for all the other fathers no longer here, but above.
We send you our thanks, red roses, and everlasting love.

61501

Take a Closer Look

"Fourteen operations in fifteen years"... I heard him say.
Laughing and bowling... I saw them play.
Giving and taking... I spent the day.
Raining and storming... they dismissed the gray.
Hoping and grateful...they knelt to pray.
Love and forgiveness...they know the way.
Kids of heart and blood and guts... not indifference, not fear, nor clay.

Through these watered eyes, I saw acceptance and family, friendship and safety.

Time is illusion.
Cancer is intrusion.
Living is confusion.
Reality is conclusion.

Metal legs and wheelchairs,
partial arms and missing hairs.
Special diets, special meds, special rules, special Keds.

Kids...rejecting seclusion.
Kids... erasing delusion.
Kids... embracing inclusion.

Battles met with courage.
Challenges met with determination.
Discovery met with innocence.
Questions met with truth.

Aspiring kids put on hold.
Young kids already old.
Shy kids being bold.
Forever kids... stories told.

Kids at odds with circumstance.
Kids forced to take a chance.
Kids viewed with a second glance.
Yet... kids still dreaming of that victory dance.

7603

The Forever Mothers

They never leave, unless to sleep.
They actually spend much more time than before...
because their children are less understood as adults.

Their gift is so special... yet so labor intense.
Their joys are so great... their concerns deep.
They never get a chance to grow old peacefully.
Yet, they grow old with love... they grow old with purpose.

TAKE YOUR HATS OFF WHEN THEY COME INTO VIEW.
Take your time and share it with these ladies.
No questions, no reasons, no explanations, no answers... just
acceptance.

Their burdens are many, their complaints are few.
They ask only understanding, they pray only for time.
While others have contact once in awhile, they are forever linked.

They march at the head of humanity's band.
They march to a greater beat.
They are the SPIRIT of creation.

121592

To Each His Own

It's been a whole 6 days.
144 hours, to be exact.
8,640 minutes, to be precise .
"You're not back to normal yet?"

I said, "My best friend died."
Not a stranger, not an enemy, not an acquaintance... my best friend.
I will be back at work.
I will be back at play.
I will be back at living.
...but, back to normal yet?

Have these people never had the displeasure of losing someone so
close?
So part of one's life? So part of one's triumphs and failures,
joys and sadness, loves and heartbreaks?

I shed a tear when fiction ends in death.
I cry when tragedy befalls the innocent.
I weep when a loved one moves away.
I tremble when a loved one is no more.
...but, back to normal yet?

In time, yes, but not measured in days, or weeks, or even years.
I will never be the same... just better for having him.
And always just a little lonelier for losing him.

I owe no explanation nor apology for my feelings.
My normal is a range of emotions, not exact nor constant.
Move on, move ahead, I will,
but you, My Friend, will be with me as I journey through life.

And I will mourn at my own pace.

12393

"I'D BE A TREE."